OTHER YEARLING BOOKS YOU WILL ENJOY:

YEARLING BOOKS/YOUNG YEARLINGS/YEARLING CLASSICS are designed especially to entertain and enlighten young people. Patricia Reilly Giff, consultant to this series, received her bachelor's degree from Marymount College and a master's degree in history from St. John's University. She holds a Professional Diploma in Reading and a Doctorate of Humane Letters from Hofstra University. She was a teacher and reading consultant for many years, and is the author of numerous books for young readers.

For a complete listing of all Yearling titles, write to
Dell Readers Service,
P.O. Box 1045,
South Holland, IL 60473.

Natalie Kinsey-Warnock
Illustrated by Leslie W. Bowman

A Yearling Book

THE CANADA GEESE QUILT

Published by
Dell Publishing
a division of
Bantam Doubleday Dell Publishing Group, Inc.
666 Fifth Avenue
New York, New York 10103

ISBN: 0-440-40719-2

Reprinted by arrangement with E. P. Dutton, a division of Penguin Books USA Inc., New York, New York, 10014

Printed in the United States of America

December 1992

10 9 8 7 6 5 4 3 2 1

CWO

For my grandmother,
Helen Urie Rowell

THE CANADA GEESE QUILT

ONE

The geese came over Miles Hill, flying low and fast, heading north. Ariel, sitting in a wild apple tree, watched them come closer, silver flashes against the dark sky. They passed over, their lonesome cries carrying to her on the cold March wind.

Ariel shivered, not so much from the cold, as from the way their song stirred her. She always watched for the geese; she almost believed that spring couldn't start until she'd heard them.

When she could no longer hear them, she climbed down and walked across the fields. Snow still lay in the hollows, but the sun had uncovered the spare brown grass on the tops of the knolls, hinting of spring. But here in the Northeast Kingdom of Vermont it would be another two months before her father could plow the fields with Lady and Jack, the gentle work horses, and begin his spring planting.

When she walked into the house, Grandma was bending over her quilting frame. She sewed with small, straight stitches.

"I saw geese today, Grandma," Ariel said.

Grandma stopped stitching and looked up.

"They're early this year," she said. "Did you sketch them?"

"No," said Ariel, "it's too cold to hold a pencil."

Ariel spent hours walking through the fields and woods, drawing wildflowers and birds. For

a year, she had kept the sketches hidden in a drawer, under her socks. It wasn't that she had thought Papa and Mama would disapprove, but they had always seemed to be talking about the war in Europe and worrying about Mama's cousin Garvin who was fighting in the Philippines. But then the war was over, Garvin was safe, and Ariel still didn't show any of the sketches to her family. One day as she sat drawing under the apple tree, Grandma had suddenly appeared.

"Why didn't you tell us you liked to draw?" she asked.

"I didn't think they were good enough," Ariel said shyly.

"Your mother wanted to be an artist," Grandma said, quietly, "but after she got married, she never painted again." She held up Ariel's drawing of a ruffed grouse.

"You have talent, Ariel, an artist's eye. Don't ever give it up." And with that encouragement, Grandma had become someone Ariel could talk to about her own dream of becoming an artist.

*   *   *

Ariel stood next to the quilting frame. The quilt was called Double Wedding Ring and Grandma had made it in shades of blue, rose, and lavender.

"Who's this quilt for, Grandma?" she asked.

"Mrs. Perkins. Her daughter's getting married."

Ariel touched the cloth lightly.

"It's beautiful," she said, "like always."

Grandma looked sideways at her.

"You want to help me with it?" she asked.

"Yuck," Ariel said, then she saw Grandma was teasing her. Grandma knew she hated to sew. But Ariel loved the quilts grandmother made. Grandma had a photo album of all the quilts she'd sold or given away. Some of her quilts were now in faraway places like Scotland and New Zealand. Papa had a Bear Paw quilt in green and brown, and Mama had two that Grandma had given to her: the Scottish Thistle had been a wedding gift, and the Iris quilt had celebrated Ariel's birth ten years ago.

Ariel reached for a cookie.

"Now don't go having your supper upside down," Grandma scolded.

"Ariel, please set the table," Ariel's mother called. She was mashing potatoes in the kettle on the stove.

"Mama, why did you stop painting?" Ariel asked.

Her mother looked startled.

"How did you find out about that?"

"Grandma told me," Ariel said. "Did Papa make you stop?"

"Heavens, no. Your father is the most understanding man I ever met."

"Then, why did you stop?" Ariel persisted.

Mama stood thinking.

"I'm not sure, really," she said. "I was so in love with your father, I guess I just got caught up with being a wife, and then a mother."

"Will you ever paint again?" Ariel asked.

"Maybe. I've found myself thinking about it lately. But I think I'll have to wait a little while longer."

"Why?" asked Ariel.
Mama smiled.
"I'll tell you after supper," she said.

_____*TWO*

After supper the family gathered around the woodstove. Mama and Papa sat next to each other, holding hands. Ariel thought her mother looked pale.

"Mama, are you sick?" Ariel asked.

Her mother laughed.

"Not exactly," she said, "but I did want to tell you and Mother something important. We're going to have a new baby around here."

Grandma sat back in her chair, a satisfied smile on her face.

"I knew it," she said to herself, but Ariel didn't even hear her. She was too stunned.

A baby! She'd asked Mama for a baby a long time ago, but Mama had just changed the subject. Now she wasn't sure she wanted a baby around. Wouldn't a baby make them all just forget about her?

Everyone was chattering away excitedly, and Ariel thought no one noticed when she slipped out to the yard. It was dark, but Ariel had climbed that apple tree so many times she could do it by touch alone. She leaned back against the trunk and felt herself drawn into the black, cold night.

The stars hung low in the frosty sky. Ariel felt she could almost reach out and touch them. She found the Big Dipper, upside down this time of year, and Cassiopeia. Her father had taught her some of the constellations. One night he'd told her a legend:

The Indians believed the stars were children

of the sun. In the morning before the sun left for work, he would put his children to bed. Then in the evening, when he came home, he would wake all his children up and set them in the sky to watch over the world while he slept. On some evenings, the sun would be so tired that he forgot to wake his children. On those nights, the sky was dark because the stars were sleeping.

The stars were not sleeping tonight. They were awake and glittering like shards of ice.

The air was so still. Ariel heard the storm door open and close and the crunch of footsteps.

"Ariel?" Grandma's voice rose through the leafless branches. "I'd like to join you up there, but I'm afraid my tree-climbing days are over."

Ariel giggled and slid to the ground. Grandma hugged her.

"Oh, Ariel," she said, "how like me you are. I used to run to the hayloft when I wanted to be alone. What if we go there and talk?"

The loft was dark and cozy. Grandma and

Ariel settled into the fragrant hay. Grandma spoke first.

"I knew you'd be feeling confused about the new baby."

"I'm just not sure how I feel about it. One part of me is glad and part of me is sad," Ariel said.

Grandma nodded.

"I remember feeling that way, too. But I had seven younger brothers and sisters, so I know what it's like to be an older sister."

"Didn't it change the way things were, Grandma?"

"Oh, I'll say it did! I never got lonely, and I didn't have much time for myself, but I'll tell you something else. I wouldn't have traded those years and those memories for anything. And when you do have brothers and sisters, why, then you can't ever imagine not having them. They can be your closest friends."

Grandma shifted position.

"I remember this hay being softer," she said ruefully. "I hate getting old."

"You're not getting old," Ariel cried, feeling suddenly protective of her grandmother.

"Thank you, honey, but of course I am," said Grandma. Her voice had a faraway sound to it. "It happened before I realized it. One day I looked in the mirror and an old woman stared back at me."

Ariel had never heard her grandmother talk like this before. Grandma was treating her like a close friend, but Ariel felt a little frightened. She didn't want to think of Grandma getting older.

"I'm sorry, Ariel," Grandma said, "I didn't mean to sound like that. What do you say we go inside and make some fudge to celebrate this new baby?"

Over the next few weeks, everyone's thoughts were on the baby. Papa whispered to Ariel that he was making a butternut cradle and asked if she wanted to help him build it. She said yes, but kept thinking about what she could do special for the baby. She could help

Papa, but the cradle would still be his present, his idea.

Nothing I do will be good enough, she thought.

She went to talk to Grandma. She felt even closer to Grandma after their talk in the hayloft.

"I know what you mean," said Grandma. "I've been wondering what I could make, too."

"You?" Ariel asked, surprised. "You can make just about anything."

"Well," said Grandma, "I wanted to make a very special quilt for the baby. But I've only made quilts from patterns my mother taught me, handed down to her by her mother. I wish this quilt could be one that nobody's ever seen before. I hoped you'd draw it."

Ariel searched Grandma's face for hints of teasing, but saw none.

"Really?" she asked. "You think I could do it?"

Grandma stroked Ariel's hair.

"I know you could. You have so much talent. And it would mean so much to everyone."

"But, Grandma, don't you see?" Ariel cried. "It's the same thing as Papa's cradle. Even if I draw the design, you'll be the one making the quilt, so it'll be your present, not mine."

"Ariel," Grandma said, "I can sew, but I can't draw. I've always wished I could but I can't. But you can design a picture that's never been made into a quilt before."

Ariel never thought of it like that. Her eyes sparkled.

Later, when Grandma went to the kitchen to start supper, she found Ariel sitting at the table, surrounded by crumpled paper.

"Looks like things aren't going so well," Grandma said.

"They're terrible," Ariel answered. "I don't know whether it's going to be a girl or boy, so I don't know what to draw."

Grandma sat thinking.

"This is going to be a special quilt because of you," she said, "so I think you should have the design show what's special to you. Why don't you think of it that way?"

Ariel worked on the drawing every afternoon

when she got home from school. The geese were still migrating north, so she took her sketchbook to the wild apple tree and watched as the geese flew over. Out here, in the raw openness, she could feel what was important to her and the design came easily.

She took the rolled drawing to Grandma's room.

"I got it done, Grandma," she said softly. She unrolled it on the bed.

On the paper, three Canada geese flew over a stand of cattails and an apple tree just in bloom. The shape of Miles Hill rose behind the tree.

Grandma didn't say anything, and Ariel said, "You don't like it, do you?"

Grandma hugged her.

"Ariel, it's wonderful," she said. "I was just a little scared. I'm not sure I'll be able to make the quilt as beautiful as that drawing deserves. Come, help me decide on the colors."

THREE

Spring came with a rush of wildflowers and soft rain. Papa was busy in the fields. Ariel planted the garden for her mother who found bending difficult. Ariel would hate the weeding later, but she did enjoy the planting: opening the brightly colored packets and pushing the seeds into the warm tilled earth.

In the evenings, Ariel helped Grandma cut out the pieces of cloth and watched as Grandma sewed them together. The quilt began to take on a life of its own, as if the geese really were rising from the cloth.

School let out in June and haying began. The most Papa would let Mama do was drive the horses ("Really, Austin," she would say, "I'm not helpless."), so Ariel worked on the wagon while Papa tossed the hay up to her. She stomped the hay down with her feet as he had shown her, so that the load held together for the bumpy ride back to the barn.

It was hot, tiring work. Ariel rushed to keep pace with her father. Sweat trickled down her back, and chaff stuck to her face and arms. Just when it seemed that the itch of the chaff would drive her crazy, they'd have a load and be riding back to the barn, a slight breeze cooling her skin. Then she could relax for a few minutes and watch red-tailed hawks circle over Miles Hill.

They got one load in just before a storm hit. Black clouds had chased them, and Mama had backed the wagon into the barn just as the

hailstones hit. While she ran to the house, Papa and Ariel unloaded the hay. The hail pelleted the roof like gunfire, so loud they couldn't speak above it. Everything seemed to glow in a strange green light.

Suddenly, Mama was standing in the doorway, her face unnaturally pale against the dark sky. There were red blotches on her arms where the hailstones had hit. Papa was beside her in an instant.

"Austin," she said, "it's Mother," and they both sprinted toward the house.

Ariel followed them, no longer aware of the storm. She'd heard the fear in Mama's voice; something was terribly wrong.

She stood on the porch, afraid to go into the house. The wind whipped at her clothes, and lightning tore jagged streaks through the sky. She shivered even though she wasn't cold.

Papa drove the car right up to the steps. He ran back into the house and, in a few minutes, he and Mama came back out, carrying Grandma. Grandma's eyes were closed, her face gray. Ariel shrank back against the porch railing. Papa lay Grandma in the back seat of the car.

Mama ducked back onto the porch and gripped Ariel's arms.

"Ariel, we have to get Grandma to the doctor. I'm counting on you to take care of yourself. Just go inside and stay there."

"Is Grandma going to die?" Ariel asked. Her voice sounded cracked and wavering.

Her mother was trying hard not to cry.

"I don't know, honey," she said. Her mouth trembled. She climbed into the back seat, cradling Grandma's head in her lap. Ariel watched the car go down the driveway and disappear over the hill. She was alone.

She wandered from room to room. Her footsteps echoed on the pine floors. The old house seemed to be holding its breath, waiting for someone to fill its emptiness.

Ariel took the Iris quilt from Mama's cedar chest. She wrapped it around herself and sat in the rocker. The picture of Grandma as she was

carried to the car played over and over in her mind. She imagined Papa and Mama coming home, both of them crying and she'd know Grandma was dead without them telling her.

Papa didn't get home until dusk. Ariel met him at the door and he gathered her up in his arms.

"Where's Mama?" Ariel asked, afraid to ask about Grandma.

"She's staying at the hospital," he said. "Grandma's very sick, and Mama doesn't want to leave her."

"I'm scared, Papa," said Ariel.

"So am I," he said, "but worrying won't help. We need to keep busy."

The days blurred together. Ariel felt numb, as if her body belonged to someone else. Mama stayed with Grandma. Meals were a strange mixture of leftovers and the few things Papa could cook. Papa and Ariel did the milking, forked hay down for the cows, curried and fed the horses, collected eggs, and tried to keep the house tidy. Papa did his best to keep Ariel's spirits up, but nothing loosened the fear that gripped her heart.

Ariel had a dream. In it, Grandma was at the cookstove, making pancakes. There was a rolled-up quilt on the table behind her. The quilt unfolded and geese began to fly out, their dark bodies filling the kitchen. Grandma raised her arms in front of her face and pushed through their beating wings. Ariel called after her, but Grandma kept walking into the darkness of their wings until she disappeared.

Ariel sat up in bed, her heart thudding. The eastern sky was just beginning to lighten.

The smell of pancakes drifted up the stairs. Ariel was out of bed in an instant, running barefoot down the stairs.

Grandma? she thought.

Mama and Papa stood by the stove, talking softly as Mama flipped the pancakes. Mama turned and saw Ariel.

"Mother's out of the woods now," she declared, brushing back tendrils of hair. She had stayed at the hospital four days, but to Ariel it seemed like months since Mama had been home. Mama had grown thinner, but that only emphasized the growing roundness of the baby. Papa hugged her.

"Claire," he said, "you've got to get some rest. You've run yourself ragged. It's not good for the baby."

Mama was too tired to protest.

"I do need some sleep," she admitted. She handed the spatula to Papa, and walked to the bedroom. Ariel followed at a distance. She watched as Mama lay down.

Mama turned over in bed, and saw her standing in the doorway. She held out her arms and Ariel rushed into them.

"I'm sorry I've been gone so much," Mama said, stroking Ariel's hair.

"When is Grandma coming home?" Ariel asked.

"Not for a long time, honey," Mama said. "She's been very sick. And even when she does come home, she'll be different."

"What do you mean, Mama?"

"Grandma had a stroke. She can't walk very well and it's hard for her to pronounce words. She's going to need all of us to help her." Mama sounded so tired. Ariel had a dozen questions to ask, but Mama was already drifting off to sleep.

_____*FOUR*

Grandma came home in August. Ariel was afraid of her. The frail, drooped-face woman in the bedroom couldn't be Grandma. Grandma had pink cheeks and busy hands; the woman in the bedroom was gray and shriveled.

Mama had said not to tire Grandma. Ariel told herself that that was the only reason she wasn't visiting with Grandma, but she knew it was more than that. She didn't like to look at

Grandma. She didn't know what to say, or how to act. Ariel spent more and more time outside, helping Papa with his work. When she did come inside, if she didn't look at that closed door, she could almost forget how everything had changed.

It was almost a relief to start school. Then Ariel didn't need to make so many excuses. With school, chores, and homework, there just wasn't any time to visit with Grandma.

Then one evening, Mama came out of Grandma's bedroom, sat down heavily in the rocker and covered her face with her hands. Papa had just come in from doing the milking and saw her.

"What's wrong, Claire?" he asked. "Is it the baby?"

She shook her head.

"Oh, Austin," she said. "Mother's given up. I thought she'd get her strength back being home. She had therapy at the hospital, and the doctor said she was able to walk with a cane now. He thought she would do better at home, but she feels she's a burden, and she isn't even trying to get better. I just don't think I can take it anymore, watching her lie there like that."

Ariel hadn't realized before that this was as hard on Mama as it was on her. And even harder on Grandma. Grandma was lying in that room, feeling that the family would be better off without her.

If it was me who was sick, thought Ariel, Grandma would do everything she could to help me.

When she got home from school the next afternoon, she took a deep breath and walked into Grandma's room. She leaned against the door wondering what she would say.

Grandma looked pale and still, nothing like the determined, energetic woman Ariel remembered.

"We had a test at school today," Ariel said, hesitantly, "and I got an *A*. We've been studying mythology. You'd read me all those stories before, anyway, remember? And I told the teacher the legend about the stars being the sun's children. She liked it."

Grandma hadn't moved or said a word. Ariel felt very uncomfortable. She knew she was rambling on to fill the silence. She sighed.

"Well, I'll see you tomorrow, Grandma," she said.

Mama met her in the hall. She hugged Ariel.

"Thank you for visiting with Grandma," Mama said. "I know it's not easy."

"Mama, I felt like I might as well be talking to an empty bed."

"I know, honey," said Mama. "But we've just got to keep on trying. Something will break through that wall she's put up."

Ariel began bringing things from her walks: an apple from her special tree, a bunch of ripe wild grapes she'd picked from the fencerow. One afternoon, she walked over to the bed, her hands cupped.

"Grandma, look!" She opened her hands; an orange monarch butterfly rested lightly on them. "I was walking home through the pasture and hundreds of butterflies flew up. Papa says they're migrating. Oh, Grandma, they were so beautiful! They filled the air." And for the first time, Ariel saw a flicker of interest in Grandma's eyes.

She's listening! Ariel thought, excitedly.

"They're still in the pasture," she said. "Let's go out and see them."

Grandma shook her head. Ariel leaned closer.

"Please, Grandma. Why have you given up? We need you. Please don't give up," she pleaded, and saw tears in Grandma's eyes.

It was a short walk. Grandma held Ariel's arm and took slow, halting steps, but there was color in her cheeks where there had been none before.

They stopped to pick chicory and Queen Anne's lace. Grandma cradled the wildflowers lovingly and looked out over the valley. The hillsides were beginning to change color. The late afternoon sun slanted across the fields. Grandma breathed the fall air deeply. For the first time since she'd been home, she looked happy.

Grandma began to talk. Her tongue moved clumsily over the words, but Ariel heard and understood them.

"I forgot life is so good," Grandma said.

When they got back to the house, Ariel lifted the quilt from its drawer and laid it in Grandma's lap.

"Now we can finish the quilt together," Ariel said.

Grandma held up her crooked hand.

"It won't be as good as if you sewed it," Ariel admitted, "but you can teach me."

Grandma gave her a questioning look.

"I know," Ariel said, laughing, "I hate to sew. And don't expect me to do it again. But this is a special occasion. Besides, you've done most of the work."

Before her stroke, Grandma had appliquéd all of the design, added a border of deep blue cloth, and started the quilting. In the past, Grandma's quick, sure fingers would have flown through the rest. Now it was up to Ariel.

Papa was filling the barn with the summer's

harvest, and Mama was so busy these days with canning and preserving the food from the garden and orchard that it was easy for Ariel to slip into Grandma's room to work on the quilt without getting questioned.

The quilting seemed agonizingly slow. Ariel made a lot of mistakes. She had to pull out stitches, and she pricked her fingers. Worst of all was sitting inside when the weather outside was so inviting.

As if to tease her, the days were especially lovely, the last warm days before the cold months of winter. The hills blazed with the scarlet and orange of maples, and the yellow of popples and birches. Apples and butternuts hung heavily from the trees along the fencerow, almost begging to be picked.

One afternoon, as Ariel walked home from school, one of the first great wedges of geese honked southward. Ariel watched them and her heart thrilled to their ancient song. She wished she was with them, sailing high and free on the wind. But Grandma was waiting.

Grandma's room seemed dark and airless compared to the deep ocean of sky and crystalline air. Ariel sat sulkily in her chair and picked up the quilt. She thought she could still hear the geese calling. She tugged at the knot in the thread until it broke, then threw the quilt to the floor.

"Oh, I'm so sick of sewing!" she cried. "A stupid quilt for a stupid baby. I'm never going to sew again. I hate it."

She jumped up and ran for the door.

"Ariel, wait," Grandma called.

Ariel spun around and before she could stop them, the words spilled out, "I want to be outside. I hate that quilt and I hate you!"

She froze in horror.

To her amazement, Grandma chuckled.

"Good for you," Grandma said in a slow, deliberate voice that was a result of her stroke. "Ever since I got home, you and your folks have been tiptoeing around here like you were on eggshells, afraid to say or do anything that might upset me. You're the first person to get mad, and I'm glad of it."

"But, Grandma, I didn't mean to say such a horrible thing. You must hate me."

"Oh, fiddlesticks, and I know you don't hate me. You're mad because I got sick and it made you scared. I get mad, too, because I can't do some of the things I used to."

Ariel ran to give Grandma a hug.

"I really love you, Grandma. And I think it's a beautiful quilt."

"But we'll both be glad when it's done, won't we?" Grandma said with a twinkle in her eye. "Run along and enjoy the afternoon. The quilt will still be here tomorrow."

After that, whenever Ariel got frustrated, she reminded herself of the battle Grandma faced. Grandma struggled with words, and with legs and hands that could no longer be trusted.

When the quilt was finally finished, Ariel was almost afraid to touch it. She'd never seen so beautiful a quilt. She and Grandma wrapped it in a sheet and stored it away in Grandma's old trunk.

_____*FIVE*

Grandma and Ariel presented the quilt to Mama on a quiet Sunday afternoon.

Mama hugged the quilt and cried.

"It's so beautiful," she kept repeating, while she stroked the cloth. "And you both made it! Mother, I'm so proud of you," she said to Grandma, then hugged Ariel extra hard.

"Thank you, Ariel," she whispered. "You gave me the best gift of all. You gave me back my mother."

Through the next few weeks, while everyone waited for the baby, life seemed to be back to normal, but for Ariel nothing would ever be the same. She and Grandma talked and, by using a cane, Grandma was able to go for short walks with her, but Ariel felt a hollowness inside. She knew now that Grandma wouldn't always be there. She tried not to think about Grandma dying, but the thought always seemed to be in her mind.

On a cold, gray morning late in October, Ariel came down the stairs to find Grandma alone in the kitchen. Grandma still slurred words and one leg dragged when she walked, but her fierce pride got her up in the morning before everyone else to start breakfast.

"Where is everybody?" Ariel asked.

"Your mother went to the hospital early this morning, Ariel," Grandma said. "The baby is on the way."

"Really? The baby's coming today?" asked Ariel. "How long will it take, Grandma?"

Grandma smiled and sighed.

"You can never tell, honey. Your dad will call us."

They kept busy all morning. Ariel fed the calves, then helped Grandma by sweeping the floors. Grandma couldn't do much housework anymore, but she could still bake. Blueberry muffins, pumpkin and apple pies, and fresh loaves of bread lined the counter.

"Grandma, what's all this food for?" Ariel asked.

"It's just to keep me busy," Grandma said. "Some people pace. I bake."

With all the chores done, Ariel found she couldn't keep her mind on anything. She dressed warmly, went to the pasture, and climbed the apple tree. The branches swayed in the wind. Slate-gray clouds raced across the sky above her.

So much had happened this year. Grandma sick, and Mama having the baby. Ariel felt like

all the worry was trying to strangle her. Why did things have to change? What if something happened to Mama, or the baby? Grandma had been sick for a long time and now was different. What will life be like when she's gone? she thought.

She had never felt so alone.

She heard them before she saw them, the haunting calls of geese in the air. They came from the north, flying ahead of the Canadian winds that would soon bring snow. Their cries touched her and her own thudding heart seemed to beat with the same steady rhythm as their wings.

They're gone again for this year, she thought. But they'll be back in the spring. How did they know to return? Year after year, they knew, even the ones that were flying the route for the first time. A knowledge passed on.

Like Grandma. Grandma had taught her things without making it seem like teaching. When to watch for the geese. Where to look for the lady's slippers and bloodroot in the swamp.

What it was like to be an older sister. How to sew a quilt even if you hated sewing.

Ariel watched the geese until they disappeared over the hills, then slowly walked home.

SIX

After the grayness outside, the kitchen seemed warm and cheery. Ariel hadn't realized how chilled she had gotten watching the geese. Grandma had lit a fire in the cookstove. A plate of fresh doughnuts sat in the middle of the table.

Grandma was smiling.

"Your dad just called," she said. "You have a brother. He and your mother are just fine. Your dad's going to take us to see them later." Ariel could see the happiness, and relief, on Grandma's face.

A brother? The word sounded so strange to Ariel. She wasn't sure what it was going to be like having a brother, but she wasn't worried about it anymore.

"Why, Ariel, you're still shivering." Grandma made her sit next to the stove and brought her a cup of hot cider.

"Now, just drink that, and I'll get you something to wrap yourself in," Grandma said, and limped to her bedroom. She reappeared within a minute, carrying a sheet-wrapped bundle. She placed the bundle in Ariel's lap.

"That should do it," she said. "Open it."

The sheet fell away. Inside was a quilt. Ariel looked at Grandma, her face showing her puzzlement.

"Is this the baby's quilt?" she asked.

"Take a closer look," said Grandma.

Ariel unfolded the quilt. There were three geese but instead of cattails, they flew over a bed of wild blue-flag iris. In the night sky, over Miles Hill and the apple tree, glittered the Big Dipper and the North Star.

Grandma's eyes sparkled like stars.

"Oh, Grandma," breathed Ariel, "is this really for me? But your stroke . . . . When did you make it?"

Grandma pulled her rocking chair close to Ariel and sat down. She touched the quilt with her stiff fingers, and spoke softly.

"When I first saw the drawing you'd made, I saw you in it. So much of what you love, and who you are, was in that drawing. I just thought the night sky suited you better. I made your quilt first, while the magic was still fresh."

Hearing all the emotion in Grandma's voice made the back of Ariel's throat ache. Then Grandma met her eyes.

"I wanted to make something special for you," she said. "I'll love that new little boy, but you're part of my heart, Ariel."

Tears welled up in Ariel's eyes.

"Don't be so afraid for me," Grandma said softly.

Ariel stared at her, unable to speak, and Grandma continued.

"I know you're afraid I'll die," she said. "But you and I must make the most of our time together. I'll always be with you, Ariel, in your memories, and in your heart. Besides," she added, smiling crookedly, "now you and I've got that boy to raise."

Grandma went back to the stove, humming as she worked.

Ariel pulled the quilt tighter around her shoulders. Wrapped in the geese, the night sky, and her grandmother's love, she felt safer than she had for a long time.